CHRISTMAS

AN AMERICAN ANNUAL
OF CHRISTMAS
LITERATURE AND ART

WINTER'S APPROACH
Water Color
Garnet Hazard

CHRIS

AN AMERICAN ANNUAL OF CHR

EDITED BY RANDOLPH E. HAUGAN • VOLUME FORTY-SIX •

TMAS

ISTMAS LITERATURE AND ART

AUGSBURG PUBLISHING HOUSE · PUBLISHERS · MINNEAPOLIS

TABLE OF CONTENTS

Volume Forty-six

First Edition

Nineteen Hundred Seventy-six

The Christmas Gospel

Christmas Articles and Stories

Christmas Poetry

Christmas Music

Christmas Art

Christmas Illustrators

Lee Mero *Audrey Teeple* *William Medcalf*
Melva Mickelson

Acknowledgments

THE LAND OF THE VISIT 16–20
Photo, pages 16, 17, Russ Busby, copyright © Billy Graham Association. Photos, pages 18, 20, Robert H. Boyd. Map, page 19, Lee Mero.

THE TREES OF CHRISTMAS 22–26
From *The Trees of Christmas*, compiled by Edna Metcalfe. Copyright © 1969 by Abingdon Press.

HOME FOR AN OLD-TIME CHRISTMAS 45-48
Currier & Ives lithographs from the Harry T. Peters Collection, Museum of the City of New York.

TRIBUTE TO A CAROL 59
From *Joys and Sorrows:* Reflections by Pablo Casals, as told to Albert E. Kahn. Simon and Schuster, Inc., New York, copyright © 1970. Photo, Puerto Rico News Service.

A MAN OF GOODWILL 65–67
Photo, page 65, Religious News Service.

LAYOUT AND DESIGN: George Nordwall

MUSIC EDITOR: Ruth Olson

Manufactured in the United States of America, Library of Congress Catalog Card No. 32-30914
International Standard Book No., Paper, 0-8066-8947-1, Cloth, 0-8066-8948-X

The Christmas Story

according to St. Luke and St. Matthew

Calligraphed & Illuminated by Judith Anne Duncan

ND IT came to pass in those days, that there went out a decree from Caesar Augustus, that all the world should be taxed. (And this taxing was first made when Cyrenius was governor of Syria.) And all went to be taxed, every one into his own city. And Joseph also went up from Galilee, out of the city of Nazareth, into Judea, unto the city of David, which is called Bethlehem; (because he was of the house and lineage of David:) to be taxed with Mary his espoused wife, being great with child. And so it was, that, while they were there, the days were accomplished that she should be delivered. And she brought forth her firstborn son, and wrapped him in swaddling clothes, and laid him in a manger; because there was no room for them in the inn. And there were in the same  ountry shepherds abiding in the field, keeping watch over their flock by night. And, lo, the angel of the Lord came upon them, and the glory of the Lord shone round about them: and they were sore afraid.

And the angel said unto them, Fear not: for, behold, I bring you good tidings of great joy, which shall be to all people. For

NTO YOU

is born this day in the city of David a Saviour, which is Christ the Lord. And this shall be a sign unto you; Ye shall find the babe wrapped in swaddling clothes, lying in a manger. And suddenly there was with the angel a multitude of the heavenly host praising God, and saying, Glory to God in the highest, and on earth peace, good will toward men. And it came to pass, as the angels were gone away from them into heaven, the shepherds said one to another, Let us now go even unto Bethlehem, and see this thing which is come to pass, which the Lord hath made known unto us. And they came with haste, and found Mary, and Joseph, and the babe lying in a manger. And when they had seen it, they made known abroad the saying which was told them concerning this child. And all they that heard it wondered at those things which were told them by the shepherds. But Mary kept all these things, and pondered them in her heart. And the shepherds returned, glorifying and praising God for all the things that they had heard and seen, as it was told unto them.

ow when Jesus was born in Bethlehem of Judea in the days of Herod the king, behold, there came wise men from the east to Jerusalem, saying, Where is he that is born King of the Jews? for we have seen his star in the east, and are come to worship him. When Herod the king had heard these things, he gathered all the chief priests and scribes of the people together, he demanded of them where Christ should be born. And they said unto him, In Bethlehem of Judea: for thus it is written by the prophet, And thou Bethlehem, in the land of Juda, art not the least among the princes of Juda: for out of thee shall come a Governor, that shall rule my people Israel. Then Herod, when he had privily called the wise men, enquired of them diligently what time the star appeared. And he sent them to Bethlehem, and said, Go and search diligently for the young child; and when ye have found him, bring me word again, that I may come and worship him also. When they had heard the king, they departed; and lo, the star, which they saw in the east, went before them, till it came and stood over where the young child was. When they saw the star, they rejoiced with exceeding great joy. And when they

were come into the house, they saw the young child with Mary his mother, and fell down, and worshipped him: and when they had opened their treasures, they presented unto him gifts; gold, and frankincense, and myrrh.

And when they were departed, BEHOLD the angel of the Lord appeareth to Joseph in a dream, saying, Arise, and take the young child and his mother, and flee into Egypt, and be thou there until I bring thee word: for Herod will seek the young child to destroy him. When he arose, he took the young child and his mother by night, and departed into Egypt: And was there until the death of Herod: that it might be fulfilled which was spoken of the Lord by the prophet, saying, Out of Egypt have I called my son···· But when Herod was dead, behold, an angel of the Lord appeareth in a dream to Joseph in Egypt, saying, Arise, and take the young child and his mother, and go into the land of Israel: for they are dead which sought the young child's life. And he arose, and took the young child and his mother, and came into the land of Israel. But when he heard that Archelaus did reign in Judea in the room of his father Herod, he was afraid to go thither: notwithstanding, being warned of God in a dream, he turned aside into the parts of Galilee: And he came and dwelt in a city called Nazareth: that it might be fulfilled which was spoken by the prophets, He shall be called a Nazarene.

The Land of the Visit

ALVIN N. ROGNESS

The greatest Visitor of all chose this land. Our Lord's coming was heralded by the angelic note of peace: "Peace among men with whom he is pleased." It was not a land of peace then, nor since. But peace came—into the hearts of hundreds of millions of people throughout the centuries. The land itself holds a fascination unique in the world.

Not since the Crusades of the 12th and 13th centuries — when the strange confluence of economic, political, and religious forces sent waves of "visitors" from the West to the holy land—have so many people, again from the West, visited the homeland of Jesus. Lured into jets by excursion fares and the promise of the customary comforts of home, this assortment of students, retired people, and Bible classes have little in common with the crusaders. Those fiery-eyed zealots set out abortively to snatch the holy places from the Arab Muslims, whose possession of the land of the Savior cried to heaven for release. The earlier "visitors" suffered hardships inconceivable to their camera-carrying descendents. Countless numbers died from disease, starvation, and the sword.

Those who trickled back, defeated and in poverty, most likely gave no lectures, illustrated or otherwise, to commemorate their exploits.

The earlier invader lived off the land; today the land lives off the invader. Tourism is a major industry of modern Palestine. Year after year, undaunted by the smoldering of the Israeli-Arab-Palestinian volcano and its sporadic bursts of fire, thousands deplane from their sleek aircraft in Tel Aviv and shuttle into the holy city, Jerusalem, to begin their bus trek to the ancient sites of Old and New Testament history. For some it is disillusioning, almost shattering, to have the pictures fed by their childhood imaginations replaced by the harsh realities, both ancient and modern, of this land. For most visitors, however, the images of their childhood come alive with enhanced vividness. Their verdict: "I wouldn't have missed it for anything."

The Old City, the city of David, is still there, about 320 acres surrounded by the great wall. Ringed with apartments of grey stone—not unlike apartment complexes of London, Moscow, or Detroit—and its sprawling new city notwithstanding, the old Jerusalem is

much the same as it was 1000 or even 2000 years ago. The Wailing Wall with its praying crowds is there. The narrow streets are flanked by innumerable small shops, through which the visitor wends his way on the *Via Dolorosa,* guided by intermittent signs on the shop walls.

Though visitors may wonder whether the Jerusalem events of the past did in fact occur at the precise sites credited to them, they can be assured that those events did after all happen within the radius of roughly a square mile. David did conquer the city from the Jebusites. Hezekiah did build the tunnel to bring water from the spring of Gihon, through which many visitors have waded, wetting their feet in the pool of Siloam where Jesus healed the man born blind.

The gold dome of Solomon's temple, rebuilt by Zerubbabel and again by Herod the Great, is now gone, and the great Mosque of Mohammed dominates the Old City. The highest spire on the skyline, however, is that of the Church of the Redeemer, built by German Lutherans in the last century.

Eastward from the walls of the Old City, separated by the brook of Kidron, is the Mount of Olives. A half hour's walk beyond brings the visitor to Bethphage and Bethany, the home of Mary, Martha, and Lazarus. To recreate the events of that last tragic and glorious Holy Week is the primary pilgrimage of most visitors. The visitor's eyes and feet follow Jesus' path

—from his triumphal entry on Palm Sunday, through the events of the Last Supper, Gethsemane, the betrayal of Judas, the denial of Peter, the fraudulent trial, Golgotha, and the empty tomb.

It is Bethlehem, five miles south of Jerusalem, that generates the tenderest emotions. There Rachel died when Benjamin was born; there Ruth came with Naomi; there David fought Goliath, and there Samuel anointed David to be king. The home of Amos and Micah the prophets, this is the village of which Micah 700 years before Christ's birth had said, "But you, O Bethlehem Ephrathah, who are little to be among the clans of Judah, from you shall come forth for me one who is to be ruler in Israel, whose origin is from of old, from ancient days" (Micah 5:2).

We who have sung Phillips Brooks' hymn, "O little town of Bethlehem, how still we see thee lie," may find it a bit difficult to substitute the stable and manger for the church now standing there. Built by Helena, mother of Emperor Constantine and dedicated in A.D. 327, in the sixth century it was enclosed by the larger structure under Justinian. But the Judean hills are there; the stars shine at night; and with a little imagination, the enchanting story of the birth, angels, shepherds, the star, and Wise Men can be reclaimed. Despite the jostling stream of pilgrim visitors and the highly ornate interior of the basilica, to stand at the bare stone entrance to the grotto is to journey back

The Bethlehem Basilica of the Nativity stands where Christ was born in a stable.

Beyond Bethlehem to the south, Joseph and Mary fled the rage of King Herod to their two-year exile in Egypt. Along this road is the area where Abraham and Lot had their farms. Here Joseph was betrayed and sold by his envious brothers. Here Absolom staged his rebellion against his father David. Hebron, probably the most ancient of the Palestinian cities, lies on the threshold of the wilderness where Moses and his people encamped for 40 years. From this point Moses dispatched spies on reconnaissance in preparation for invasion of the promised land. Before the conquest of Jerusalem, it was David's royal city. Abraham, Sarah, Isaac, and Jacob are reputed to be buried here.

some 2000 years to that quiet event which changed the world. God, God the Son, had come as the Messiah, long promised, to redeem the world.

Bethlehem is but one of the intriguing goals of the modern traveller. Busses whisk people through this land that stretches along the Mediterranean coast. About 150 miles long, at its widest point Palestine is but 70 miles wide. About two-thirds of the area lies west of the astonishing Jordan River, which plunges from the 9000-foot Mount Hermon down an ever-deepening gorge to the brackish depths of the Dead Sea, 1300 feet below sea level.

All through ancient history the more powerful nations had coveted and intermittently conquered this corridor of trade between East and West. Richly laden caravans of camels, donkeys, and horses, moving to and from Mediterranean ports, meandered through this trade route. And the small country, since the reign of David no match for its stronger neighbors, became almost continuously a vassal of the powerful, its people often driven into exile or captivity.

In spite of this touch-and-go existence, God held the people together, often no more than a remnant. But they were never swallowed up. Historians have puzzled over the phenomenon of this people retaining an indigestible identity, though deprived of geographic sovereignty and persecuted to the death again and again. Its present brief and tenuous independence as a nation is the first since the sack of Jerusalem by Rome in A.D. 70.

Most of the visitors to Palestine today are not as interested in the new state as they are in seeing the ancient landmarks, the places they have learned to know through the Bible. The tourist busses fan out like the spokes of a wheel from Jerusalem as the hub, south to Bethlehem and Hebron, east to Jericho and the Dead Sea, and north to Galilee. Guides accompanying the busses, whether Christian, Israeli, or Arab, tell the story of the country, both ancient and modern.

East from Jerusalem, on to Jericho and the Dead Sea, visitors are reminded of Jesus' story of the Good Samaritan as they pass an inn by that name. Jericho, a lush oasis in an otherwise barren terrain of rock-covered hills, recalls Joshua and the collapse of the walls of Jericho. Here, too, Zacchaeus climbed the tree to see Jesus. On to the Jordan river, where Jesus was baptized by John. Nearby is the desolate wilderness, thought to be the place of the temptation of Jesus. And in the nearby hills is the Jebel Qarantal area, where in recent years a young Bedouin shepherd boy stumbled upon the famed Qumran ancient scrolls. Reaching the Dead Sea, many visitors swim in the salt-laden water which keeps them floating like corks on its surface.

It is the northbound spoke of the wheel that usually delights travellers the most. The Sea of Galilee, Capernaum, Nazareth, Cana—all bring alive the more pleasant episodes in the life of Jesus. The memories of Jerusalem are grim; thoughts of Galilee, if not totally happy, are at least pleasant.

The whole countryside is verdant with fertile fields and vineyards, wild flowers and birds. Nazareth, on the southern slope of Jebel es-Sikh, has a commanding view of snow-crowned Mount Tabor. Below are stands of pine, palm, and fruit trees, fields of grain. Off to the east lies the beautiful Sea of Galilee and Capernaum, the city of Jesus' frequent ministries. If other things have changed in 2000 years, at least nothing has altered the Sea of Galilee, where Jesus recruited the fishermen Peter, James, and John, and where he so often appeared to his disciples. On the nearby hillside he probably preached and fed the 5000.

Along the coast are the ports of Caesarea, Joppa, Tyre, Sidon—names associated with Paul more than with Jesus. Haifa is a modern port of commerce. Inland along major roadways are the resort cities of Caesarea Philippi and Tiberius, names that go back to Roman occupation.

THE LAND of THE FIRST CHRISTMAS

The visitor wends his way on the *Via Dolorosa*, following the path of Jesus.

Since 1947, when Israel became a sovereign state by the mandate of the United Nations, Jewish refugees and entrepreneurs from around the world have come. Most of them are determined to make this their homeland. With their characteristic competence and with the aid of foreign capital, they have made great strides in industry and in reclaiming arid land for forests, for grazing, for fruit, and for grain. Communal living, the kibbutz, is an experiment in cooperative endeavor which has had general acceptance.

For many years the area of Palestine had a large Arab population, and it still has, in spite of the arrival of Jewish people. Rivalries of long standing complicate the life and jeopardize the peace of this new government. Certainly Palestine is one of the many places in our world where the ability of diverse classes and religions to live together peaceably and with mutual enterprise is currently being tested.

The guide will doubtlessly point out Golan Heights, the precarious mountain crest from which, on both sides, vigilant armed forces are on watch to avert invasion. As the bus stops to let the visitors look at some abandoned and demolished tank from the 1967 or 1973 wars, a moment of apprehension overwhelms the group, as if at any moment some new violence may break out. Occasional planes streak overhead, adding, if not fear, at least uneasy glamor to the hour. Some may even try a camera shot. It is an unreal, and yet very real, contemporaneous world.

And there is Masada. Hardly any bus tour will overlook this citadel of ancient valor. The guide will

tell this story of the first century, how Rome swept through the country, finally marooning and besieging the remaining 4000 Jews on the heights of Masada. Knowing that on the next day they were doomed to conquest and slavery, they entered into a death-pact. When the Romans reached the plateau at the top, they found only the dead. Everyone—men, women and children—had chosen death rather than slavery or execution. Israel's present passion for independence is not unaffected by the legend of Masada.

Whether a person is disposed to interpret biblical prophecy in a direct manner, or whether he is a realistic student of modern international affairs, this little plot of ground looms with strategic importance. The biblicist may recall the prophecies of an Armageddon and conclude that here, in this corner of the world, the final showdown of demonic and divine forces will occur; and that here, perhaps in Jerusalem, the Lord will make his second coming. The statesman of the 20th century, quite apart from any biblical reference, senses that the issues that agitate this corner of the world may draw into a vortex a gigantic confrontation of the great powers of our day.

For in 1947 feelings of suspicion and age-old hostilities did surface between Arab people who had long occupied this land and the new immigrants. Approximately 1.5 million people of Arab background, known now as Palestinians, consider themselves refugees, people seeking both a status and a geography, and driven often to violence and harassment to achieve their ends. The Jewish immigrants in turn, victims of the more recent brutal Nazi horror and of centuries-long persecution, feel that the nations of the world owe them support in returning to their long-lost homeland.

Valiant efforts are made on all sides to find a way for these people to live together in peace and freedom. Former Prime Minister Golda Meier never used the term *enemy* in referring to the Arabs, but always *neighbors*. Many leaders among the Arabs, now united in a pro-Arab world after 1000 years of disunity, are seeking ways to accept the new nation as a permanent piece in the mosaic of the Near East.

Jerusalem is the focus of three of the great religions of the world, Christian, Judean, and Mohammedan. Religious convictions and passions run deep and generate forces not easily governed by political realities. But even these religions, in a world shrunken to a little island, more and more are finding ways of dealing with one another with charity and respect, using the tools of persuasion instead of coercion.

Perhaps God, who chose to make his one visible appearance on earth in this land, will use it again to reveal himself anew as the Lord of love, and to remind us all that he is indeed the Father "from whom every family in heaven and earth is named." If it can happen here in microcosm, in this land of diversity, perhaps it can happen the world over.

christmas poem for my daughter

His tiny fingers
pull at packaged mystery—
parable of life.

Sleep child, God bless you—
strengthen you to touch with grace
God's aching, hurt world.

"I love you so much"—
unwritten on gift or card,
yet wordlessly said.

Haiku by Wilson C. Egbert

For your first Christmas
child
I'd give you many things:
turquoise powder
from butterfly wings
caramel kisses in
fields of wild honey
ribbons scarlet as
autumn maple leaves
speckled scales
from silver-bellied fish
rainbows
in droplets of water
silk
yellow as sunflowers
milkweed floss
to tickle your nose

All these things
I'd love to give you
but since they fade
wrinkle or fall
let me give you
endless love
from One
who on this day
became a child like
yourself

Hugh Cook

The Trees of Christmas

Like the season itself, the Christmas tree is a delightful mixture of fact and folklore, the simple and the sophisticated. Each tree creates a distinctive mood and takes you on a colorful journey into the magic of the holidays.

Christmas was unknown in Japan until a century ago. Today the Christian population celebrates the day with religious meaning, and it has also become a popular holiday for those who do not profess Christianity.

When the Christmas season approaches, there is great activity in the stores. In the cities one sees festive decorations, even Christmas trees with lights and ornaments and Santa Claus with reindeer. Shoppers throng the streets, creating a year-end business boom which has been actively encouraged by merchants. There is a great spirit of gaiety as more and more Japanese express interest in Christmas as a holiday season.

This is not surprising in a country where festivals have been part of civilization for 1000 years. Some are religious festivals of a faithful people, some celebrate an event in history or honor an ancient scholar. Many are for children. The great love of the Japanese for children is manifested in such days as Girls' Day, Boys' Day, and Big Kite-flying Day.

The manufacture of Japanese goods for the Christmas markets of the world and an ever-increasing communication with other countries has combined with this love of children to popularize Christmas. Christmas trees are decorated with small toys and dolls, fluted paper ornaments, and candies in gay wrappings.

New Year's Day is the most keenly enjoyed and widely celebrated event of the Japanese calendar. Many of the practices of this season resemble those of the Western world at Christmas. There is a thorough housecleaning, and traditional decorations of pine, bamboo, and apricot are used. The *kadomatsu* (gate pine) is set on either side of the front entrance; this is a decoration not seen at any other time of the year. Special food is eaten during the holiday, and friendship is the keynote of the season. Calls are made to homes of friends, relatives, and business acquaintances, and gifts of all kinds are given.

In Japan, the second night of the New Year is a time for foretelling the future for those who believe in dreams. New Year festivities in Japan continue with various events until January 20th.

Japan

The Christmas season is joyful and busy in Denmark. The people consider Christmas their greatest festival of the year and enjoy elaborate preparations for its observance. Christmas Eve is a time of chiming church bells, family dinner, the ceremony around the tree, and hymns and carols in candle-lit churches.

The first harbinger of the season is the great Baking Day. Every Danish home becomes virtually a bakery about the middle of December, but Baking Day is something special. On that day the housewife mixes the dough for *brunekage*, a paper-thin spice cookie served in all Danish homes at Christmas. The mixing is done two or three weeks before the baking so that the dough may ripen and the flavors meld. A recipe given by a Danish housewife will yield three or four hundred cookies, for in this hospitable country one must have a plentiful supply of food.

On Christmas Eve the family gathers for an early meal. The Danish flag decorates the home as well as the Christmas tree. The lighted candle in the window offers food and shelter to travelers who may be passing, in the spirit of the Christ child. As the twilight falls, the father reads the Christmas gospel, and in the darkening room the family sings the Christmas songs dear to their hearts, such as the one by their own poet Hans Brorson:

> Thy little ones, dear Lord, are we
> And come thy holy bed to see.
> Enlighten every soul and mind
> That we the way to thee may find.

The first course of the dinner is the traditional rice pudding with a whole almond in it. The one who finds the almond keeps the others in suspense until all the porridge is eaten. Then he announces his prize triumphantly and claims the reward— usually a fruit of marzipan. The rest of the dinner consists of goose stuffed with apples and prunes and served with red cabbage, potatoes, and lingonberry sauce.

After dinner is over, the father and mother disappear into the locked parlor or living room. Then the doors are suddenly flung open, and there is the gleaming Christmas tree. The youngest child is the first to enter the room, then all the family clasp hands and circle round the tree singing Danish songs and carols.

On Christmas Eve when the rice pudding is served, a bowl of pudding is ceremoniously set aside for the *nisse,* a barn elf or sprite who keeps a friendly eye on the animals in the barn or other domestic animals in town or country.

Denmark

The Tree of Jesse

The Christmas tree, glowing with light and topped by a shining star or an angel, symbolizes Christ as the Light of the world and brings the true message of Christmas. The Tree of Jesse, with its symbols representing Old Testament stories and events leading up to the birth of Christ, is another approach to the meaning of Christmas.

The representation of the Tree of Jesse is based upon the prophecy of Isaiah 11:1-2: "And there shall come forth a rod out of the stem of Jesse, and a branch shall grow out of his roots: and the spirit of the Lord shall rest upon him." In works of art, the genealogy of Christ is frequently shown in the form of a tree which springs from Jesse, the father of David, and bears as its fruit the various ancestors of Christ.

The Jesse Tree symbols transform a Christmas tree into a "family tree" of Christ, since each ornament is a symbol of an ancestor or of a prophecy which foretells his coming. The symbols are the sun, the tablets of the Law, the key of David, Bethlehem, the root of Jesse, Noah's ark, the Ark of the Covenant, the altar of holocaust, the apple, the paschal lamb, the pillar of fire, manna, the star of David, Jacob's ladder, Jonah in the whale, the temple, the crown and the scepter, the sword of Judith, the burning bush.

The sun represents Christ as bringing eternal life and light, and is based on the prophecy of Malachi: "But unto you that fear my name shall the Sun of righteousness arise with healing in his wings." The six-pointed Star of David symbolizes the lineage of Christ from the royal house of David. The burning bush symbolizes the virgin birth, and the prophecy of the birth is seen in the Bethlehem emblem. The apple is a symbol of Christ, who took upon himself the burden of man's sin, and Jacob's ladder is interpreted as Christ reuniting mankind to God.

The Jesse Tree was an early form of design for the stained glass windows of great cathedrals, such as Chartres. The twisting branches of the tree always start with Jesse and end at the top with Christ. The Tree of Jesse window in the cathedral at Chartres is full of meaning and symbolism. In the lowest panel Jesse is lying upon a couch; from his loins rises the stem of a tree which branches out into scrolls enclosing seated figures of the sons of Jesse holding the branches. Next to the upper panel is the virgin; the upper panel holds the figure of Christ, much larger, with the dove descending from above.

Christmas Eve is one of the most important family holidays of the Lithuanians. It is a day of peace, good will, religious recollection, and intimate family reunion. Members of the family fast all day as they prepare for *Kucia*, the Christmas Eve dinner, highlight of the day, and for *Kaledos*, Christmas Day.

The home is cleaned thoroughly, and holiday foods fill the house with tantalizing aromas. After the chores are done, members of the family scrub in the *pirtis* (steam bath) and don holiday garb. The Christmas Eve table is spread with sweet fresh hay and covered with a handloomed snowy linen cloth reserved for the occasion. A crucifix and a plate of holy wafers are placed in the center of the table. When the evening star appears in the sky, the head of the family begins the meal with a prayer of thanksgiving for past blessings and a wish that the family remain intact during the coming year. He breaks and shares the holy wafers with each member of the family, and they, in turn, with each other.

The Christmas Eve menu consists of 12 courses which commemorate the 12 apostles, but no meat is served. Soup, fish, vegetables, a small hard biscuit served with poppy-seed and honey sauce, and an oatmeal pudding are included. The meal is leisurely, and conversation centers on the significance of Christmas.

In some sections of Lithuania the *Kucia* table is not cleared of food, lest the Christ child and his mother visit during the night. It is also believed that souls of deceased members of the family might return briefly—and they must find a hospitable table. The floor is carefully swept so there will not be even a crumb on which a visitor might stumble.

Christmas Eve is a time when old superstitions foretelling the future are enjoyed. Straws are drawn from under the tablecloth to determine the length of life—or in case of young people, the length of their single life. The future can be seen in the shape of molten lead, wax, or fat poured into cold water, for legend says that it changes into wine on this night; or they run to the barn to capture the mystic moment when the animals have the power to speak.

The hay from under the tablecloth, together with choice bits of *Kucia* food, is given to animals in gratitude for their work and in appreciation of the thought that animals in the stable guarded and warmed the holy Child in Bethlehem.

Lithuania

In Italy the Christmas season lasts for three weeks, beginning eight days before Christmas and ending with Twelfth Night. The Christmas celebrations center around the birth of the baby Jesus, and a *presèpio,* or manger, is prepared in every home. Members of the family offer prayers and light candles every morning. As a result of this concentration on the significance of Christmas, Italy has not adopted the Christmas tree to any extent, and the joviality of the northern holiday is absent.

The manger scene which emphasizes the meaning of Christmas was originated by St. Francis of Assisi. In the village of Greccio in 1223 he arranged a manger with hay. Using live animals and the people of the village, he depicted the scene at Bethlehem in such a way that the people with their own eyes could see the privation suffered by the holy family. St. Francis arranged for Mass to be celebrated at this nativity scene. Many people came to Greccio, along with the brothers of St. Francis, and the songs and service around the crib filled their hearts with joy at renewing the mystery of the nativity.

Following St. Francis, manger scenes were set up in churches, and people brought gifts to the holy infant. Later the crib became the inspiration of artists and craftsmen who made miniature scenes for their own homes. The popularity of this custom spread to the court, and nobles and kings hired artists to produce lavish scenes. Many figures were added representing various social classes, all clad in the dress of the day. Always the *presèpio* in the Italian home has been the center of interest, and the figures are carefully treasured. Some are generations old and perhaps handmade by a member of the family. The nativity scene appears also in shop windows, in windows of houses, and even in open doorways.

Frequently the manger scene, laid out in the shape of a triangle, is the base for the *ceppo,* a light wooden frame arranged as a pyramid. Several tiers of shelves are supported by the framework, and the whole structure is decorated with colored paper and gilded pine cones, with candles at the corners of the shelves. The shelves above the crib scene hold candy, fruit, or small presents. In some homes there is a *ceppo* for each child in the family. The *ceppo* is in the tradition of the Tree of Light, which became the Christmas tree in other countries. It is thought that it originated as a substitute for the Yule log and that the pyramidal form represents the flames.

Italy

Our Christmas Heritage

LA VERN J. RIPPLEY

Illustrated by William Medcalf

SWITZERLAND

Although the feast of Christmas was "born" in Bethlehem, the cradle that rocked it was the transalpine region of Europe. With its rich pre-Christian folklore and its tendency toward cultural amalgamation, northern Europe became the mother's knee which nurtured Christmas into the mature tradition we commemorate annually. Not in Italy, the fatherland of Christianity, nor even in Rome, its hometown, has Christmas been so richly embellished as in northern Europe.

There must be an explanation why Norway, Sweden, England, Germany, Denmark, Scotland, and neighboring northern lands produced the hybrids of tradition that were carried around the globe by emigrants from these countries. Historically, the date of Christ's birth is unknown. For centuries the event was little more than a mother and child in search of a birthday. According to some, the early Christians stressed the divinity of Jesus to such an extent that they repressed from history not only the date of Jesus' birth, but also even the fact of his becoming man. Given this theological framework, Christmas was more of a bane than a boon to converts from paganism.

In early Christian Rome, the end and the beginning of each year was celebrated by the *saturnalia*—a time when raucous Romans made merry, masqueraded through the streets, ate big dinners, and exchanged gifts. To the Christians, these boisterous activities were an abomination. Not only that, they were associated with pagan worship. Because the 10-day *saturnalia* festival commemorated the last days of the ebbing sun and the first days of its rebirth, Christians said the Romans were worshipping the sun. High tide of these festivities came at the low point in darkness—roughly, the 25th of December.

When Christianity moved north several centuries later, its stern antipaganism had mellowed toward existing cultures. As a result, a new symbiotic relationship between the pre-Christian customs of the northern European tribes and the commemoration of Christ's birth led to combining the feasts of the sun's and the Lord's rebirth. The task of transmitting Christianity north of the Alps, furthermore, was in the hands of natives of the North who had been trained in Rome. For example, St. Boniface came from the Anglo-Saxons of England, studied in Rome, and went as a missionary to the Saxons of Germany. St. Olaf was not only the propagator of the Christian faith, but did so forcibly because he was also the king of Norway. St. Patrick probably came from England, studied in France, and went as a missionary to the Emerald Island. (Continued on page 30)

27

NORWAY

AUSTRIA

Perhaps the most significant factor that affected the celebration of Christmas in northern Europe was the climate. Around the end of the year, it is always cold there, if not universally snow-blanketed. Settled by immigrants who came predominantly from northern Europe, the United States too has traditions which depict the Christmas season as cold and snowy. Virtually all of our fantasies concerning the real event of Christ's birth presuppose bitter winter. The use of evergreens, candles, and torches may date back to Roman times, but the true significance of the "death of the sun" probably was not felt by Christians until the missionaries experienced it in the north. There the nights were much longer than in Italy, Greece, Egypt, or the Middle East. The days were colder, the clouds heavier, and the atmosphere more brooding. The Germanic tribes had no way to measure the solstices and equinoxes, we are told, but they certainly experienced the climatic variances.

Our traditions of dining at Christmas also stem from the northern European countries rather than the Mediterranean. Turkey is an American invention, but the goose was Christmas fare for centuries in northern Europe. Wealthier households also enjoyed swans, venison, and boar's head. The boar figured in ancient Scandinavian yuletides. Boars were considered sacred by the Norsemen and the Celts and thus were quite literally assimilated into the medieval Christmas. Although boar is no longer a part of the Christmas fare, the mince pies, raisins, fruits, spices, nuts, and various versions of plum puddings have decked both medieval and modern tables. In Catholic areas and in Scandinavia, the vigil of Christmas is observed by eating fish at the Christmas Eve meal. Germans like carp and northern Italians prefer stewed eels, while the Norwegians cling to their dried cod soaked in lyewater, otherwise known as lutefisk.

A joyous and charming part of many a north European Christmas is sharing fruits of the fields with animals. German families in the Pennsylvania Dutch area feed their cattle and horses extra rations on Christmas Day. In Germany, as well as in German-American rural areas, farmers take wheat and oats along to church on Christmas Day and afterwards feed it to the cattle, not only as a special treat, but also as protection against sickness and evil during the long winter. In Swedish villages a sheaf of grain is positioned on a wheel on top of a high pole for bird feeding. South Germans strew seeds on rooftops; though this has not caught on in America, the Norwegian tradition of posting a bundle of wheat for the birds has. In the upper Midwest this Norwegian custom allows a few Minnesota farmers to bind their entire crop into sheaves for sale to Christmas bird-watchers. Perhaps these splendid traditions were derived from St. Francis of Assisi who legitimized our inborn sympathies towards the animal kingdom at Christmastime.

St. Francis is sometimes also credited with inventing the crèche. In reality, his display at Greccio in 1223 exhibited none of the fixtures and figures, with the exception of an empty manger, that are now associated with the crèche. The crèche too is a north European development. It too presupposes a severe winter climate which made shelter a necessity for the mother and child. It also presupposes the time in history when the theater came into prominence. Both of these conditions prevailed in the middle Alpine district of Europe late in the 16th century.

Franciscan mysticism incorporated the animal world into the theology of salvation. In the Alps, with the winter as catalyst, this new harmony of nature and spirit blended well. Shelter conceived in its purest form was not man-made in the city, but God-given in the countryside. In other words, the finest refuge was a simple barn warmed by the breath of animals. Hence, the birth of the crèche.

It is also no accident that the crèche became a far-flung tradition during the period of baroque art, which had a penchant for portraying abstract theology in visible form. At the same time, theater enjoyed a heyday, not only in England but also in Bavaria and Austria, exactly where the crèche was gaining the greatest popularity.

The crèche is folk art. It is also the livelihood of entire towns in southern Germany. Oberammergau and Garmisch-Partenkirchen are thriving commercial centers, not because of winter sports traffic nor even because the Passion Play is staged there every decade, but because of the wood-carving skills of the local people. Virtually all of them are engaged in carving wooden figures for Christmas crèches. Parenthetically it should be noted, however, that the 400-year-old passion play tradition in Oberammergau is but another manifestation of the willingness of Alpine burghers to depict their faith in theatrical dimensions. Whether viewing the crèche or the Passion Play, we are reliving the most central phenomena of the Christian religion —the birth and death and resurrection of Jesus.

From the Alpine centers of Bavaria and Austria, the crèche was transported by the Jesuits to Czechoslovakia and northern Europe. Always these priests stressed the pedagogical—what we might call the use of visual aids—when carrying the gospel to the faithful. At a later period German immigrants brought the crèche to America. Its transplantation on American soil may well have born less fruit, however, if the Jesuits had not been expelled from Germany in the 19th century, leaving them no choice but to pick up their visual aids and accompany their countrymen to our shores.

Christmas carols, unlike the crèche, did not have a religious origin. They grew out of medieval ring dances which were accompanied by songs with a secular theme. Usually they told of love, courtship, feasting, the return of spring, or some other cheerful event. Christmas hymns were known long before carols came

(Continued on page 33)

DENMARK

SWEDEN

into being, but they dealt with the theology rather than the emotional aspects of Christ's incarnation. Scottish highlanders played carols on bagpipes and English country folk sang them while moving from house to house on dark wintry nights. Then as now, Christmas carols expressed happiness with spontaneous emotion. Since the Puritans disapproved of emotional song, carols were driven out of English churches and city homes. As a result, Christmas carols did not return to the English home nor the church until the middle of the 19th century. On the continent, of course, the tradition of caroling in and out of churches was never interrupted.

Due to America's strong Puritan heritage, Christmas carols were brought from Germany and the Scandinavian countries rather than from Great Britain. Neither the crèche, the Christmas carol, nor for that matter the secular theater found much acceptance in the United States until the colonial traditions of Puritanism had been diluted by a tidal influx of non-English immigrants in the decades after 1840. Thereafter, the words and melodies passed from generation to generation and from foreign language to English tongue, until today Americans have the richest assortment of Christmas carols in the world.

The Christmas tree, although thoroughly embedded in Swedish tradition, did not originate there. In Sweden, where the winter nights are even longer and the summers shorter than on the European mainland, the evergreen dominated the landscape and spoke to the primitive mind with a symbolic language of sunshine and summer. Actually the tradition of erecting a Christmas tree in the home originated in Strassburg, Germany—now eastern France. Soon it spread throughout all of the German-speaking lands. Most scholars agree that the custom of decorating Christmas trees was brought to colonial America in the mid-18th century by German settlers in Pennsylvania and Virginia, and subsequently by the Hessian soldiers who were hired by the British to fight in the American Revolutionary War. The Christmas tree did not arrive in England until the 19th century when immigrants from Germany came to the Manchester area, and it did not become popular there until the 1840s.

Like the crèche, the Christmas tree is strictly a product of northern Europe. At first dried fruits decorated it, but eventually candles, tinsel, and glittering balls were substituted. Placing candles on the tree has continued throughout history, and in Europe, where traditions die harder, families still have not abandoned their love of the authentic flame in favor of something less hazardous. Bred by the climatic forces of northern Europe, the Christmas tree has taken root in our American South as well as the North, but everywhere in the United States the winter motif accompanies it.

Bringing Christmas to America resulted in an amalgamation. Pagan and Christian traditions reached a new land, though not exactly a virgin land, for the American Indians had also celebrated the year-end change of seasons much as primitive man everywhere had done. Through an eclectic process, diverse traditions from European countries were assimilated into our own national Christmas. Only in stronger enclaves of Germans, Swedes, Danes, and Norwegians, or in the worship of Russian Orthodox, Moravians, and Catholics, have the European flavors remained dominant.

Occasionally in the United States, moreover, one finds customs which long ago disappeared from the European parentland but which are "fossilized" for posterity in America. The highlanders of the Ozarks, for instance, cling to their date of Old Christmas Day in January, which disappeared in England during the 18th century. Certain European peasant stock in Kentucky still roam about on Christmas Eve banging on anything from a frying pan to a coal shovel, a custom formerly typical of Europeans on Christmas but practiced today only on New Year's Eve.

Traditions from the old country also changed significantly in the new. In the American South, the Yule log turned into the "Christmas log." It thrived on institutional slavery. As long as the Christmas log was burning, tradition permitted the slaves to make merry, free of any duties. Tired slaves soon learned to sprinkle it with water to keep it burning as long as possible.

In Philadelphia on New Year's Day, the mummers parade with an ebullience that takes us back to pagan celebrations. Other American cities used to have parades to commemorate the winter solstice, but the carousing often got out of hand and police intervention finally obliterated most of them. In North Carolina the masquerading theme is perpetuated when two men draped with a sheet and a steer's head go flapping down the street. Known as "Old Buck," this Christmas tradition too is a carry-over from primitive religions. In New Orleans it lives in the shape of a real ox parading at Christmastime with holly on its beribboned horns.

All of these Christian traditions and natural rituals which descended to America pale in comparison to the great supernatural event that is commemorated in the churches, the hearths, and the hearts of millions during the festival of Christ's nativity. When Dutch immigrants first introduced Santa Claus to New Amsterdam, they were perpetuating the memory and the benevolent acts of a kindly bishop. Today he is heavily overlaid with the Scandinavian tradition of a kindly elf. For many Americans, he is neither bishop nor elf but a commercial symbol. The tree, the masquerades, the carols, the Yule log, the candles, mistletoe, and wreaths, while commercialized as well, are all derived from pre-Christian folk belief. Yet who would suggest that these ancient pulsations in our bloodstream at Christmas time should be abolished. For all the traditions together compel us to let go our petty reality in order to grasp at the spirit. Everything earthy and ancient bears fruit at that one moment when we take the gamble and grasp at the vision in hopes of experiencing a morsel of the Invisible.

ENGLAND

AN OLD SCRAPBOOK brings back Memories of CHRISTMAS in the Past

A Picture Story by LEE MERO

I remember, I remember
How my childhood fleeted by
The mirth of its December
And the warmth of its July.

Mr. Winthrop Mackworth Praed 1802-1834 wrote those words

CHRISTMAS-TIME

always seems to bring back memories of bygone holidays, happy times, childhood recollections.

To those who like to recall "The Mirth of its December" we present these pages.

The Editor and the artist

This sort of card was popular the year that Uncle August brought his family up to the city to spend the holidays with Henry's folks.

BA-NAN-AS!!!

Dave Carstens, Engineer on No. 4

That was little Herbert's first train ride and he proved to be a pint-sized Business Stimulator for the "news butcher."

The City offered one surprise after another! Uncle August rode out in front on a horse car and visited with an old neighbor who had come to town just the year before while Aunt Esther and Bud enjoyed the comfort inside

JAYWALKER!

BEAVER & KNUDSON FURNITURE

AW, CHESTNUTS

They didn't mind the weather because of their nice warm Buffalo Coats!

Little Abigail, whose folks had farmed the quarter-section next to Uncle August's, was now a cash girl in Goodfellow's Dry Goods Store

your change ma'm

WICK
SECOND AISLE MADAM

Curfew shall NOT ring tonight!

And her sister Maud was also in the city, taking elocution lessons

Aunt Carrie sort o' wished August might have some of that floor walker's CHARM, but then—it wouldn't help much following a plow.

To get "spruced up" for the holidays the men went over to Nelson's Barber Shop where Uncle August was treated to a shave, being "lathered up" from Uncle Henry's own Individual Mug!

With all the Compliments of THE SEASON

Turkey a la promenade

Mr Nasby (Manager of Peterson & Schmidt Butcher Shop) sent this card to his customers THE YEAR that Henry's family went back home to spend Christmas on the farm

Junior had ridden in elevators & horse cars But the trip in the Caboose of the slow freight on the branch line to Jewell added to "the Mirth of his December!"

They arrived at the village along with lutefisk, nuts (and bolts), molasses, farm implements, flour, etc., etc., etc.,—

FELLOW TRAVELERS

Ol' 199 was all steamed up over the holidays

Seemed as if it was yet night when Aunt Delores coffee grinding began And little Barbara peered from her window to see Uncle Albert already on his way to the barn for the early morning chores!

CRUNCH GRIND CRUNCH

THERE WAS ALWAYS SOMETHING COOKING DURING THE HOLIDAYS

After breakfast, Jonathan, who had always been a Consumer, was introduced to the PRODUCERS

David

(a requested reprint)

THE SHEPHERDS
Richard I. Heule

Home for an Old-time Christmas

TOM MACPHERSON

A "Winter Evening"

Currier & Ives

It is a new Christmas every December 25th, but it is always an old-time Christmas, with warm traditions that bring home those of us who had gone off to school or to faraway jobs.

In the early years of the 19th century, "home for Christmas" usually meant just waking up on Christmas morning. Few Americans traveled far in those days, when horsepower was the horse itself. Those who traveled were pushing the frontier westward or answering the call of the gold fields, but they were few, and would not be expected to make it home each year.

In the latter third of the century there were railroads, and sons of some families left home to "seek their fortunes." The same train that took a son away often would bring him home for the holidays. This December, wherever on the continent sons and daughters may be, all can reach home within one or two days' travel, and most do. Extra buses and extra air-planes, and even the ailing railroads, will be hauling throngs of us home for that old-time Christmas.

In four out of five homes we will find a decorated Christmas tree. The tree itself may be plastic, making some of us wistful or critical—mumbling about the "traditional live evergreen." Yet, as traditions go, American Christmas traditions are young and are put together in the same manner as our population—from many lands, mostly European.

The first Christmas tree was brought here by Germans; the singing of carols originated in Italy and came to us via England; the Scandinavians taught us to make gingerbread men and other cookies for decorating the tree. These and other Christmas practices were established while two remarkable chroniclers were publishing a pictorial record of 19th-century America. The two chroniclers were Nathaniel Currier and James Merritt Ives.

45

An ice-boat race on the Hudson river.   *Currier & Ives*

Newspapers were rare in the early years of the 19th century, and photography was still in its infancy. A few craftsmen were laboring with lithography, the new method for printing copies of paintings or drawings. Events of the day would be chronicled in lithographs, which were sold to the general public for 15 to 25 cents each.

When Nathaniel Currier was 15 he was apprenticed to a lithographer in Boston. The successful lithographer was a combination of artist and tradesman. He always painted or sketched his scene on a special type of stone, and transferred it to a second stone in order to reverse the scene from left to right. Prints were made from the second or negative stone, and were thus reversed to agree with the original scene.

Although he never became much of an artist, Nathaniel Currier learned his trade well enough to set himself up in business after five years of apprenticeship. His first shop was in Philadelphia, but he soon moved to what is now the capital of the printing world, New York City. He was 22 years of age.

In December of that year, 1835, a disastrous fire destroyed several acres of New York's business district. Within four days the young Mr. Currier was selling lithograph prints of his *Ruins of the Merchants' Exchange*. As four days was remarkably fast time to be out on the street with prints, Currier sold thousands of copies.

In later years Currier's name, linked with that of Ives, would be more famous as a signature beneath genteel scenes of the outdoor aspects of America, but the Currier shop prospered originally by illustrated reporting of major events, and such events were, more often than not, tragic. By the time Currier took his bookkeeper, James Ives, into partnership, they were

also finding many buyers for prints of deathbed portraits of famous people.

As one successful year followed another, Currier and Ives turned out lithographs of just about everything on the 19th-century American scene. Occasionally they would select a day in history, as they did with the print: *Surrender of General Burgoyne at Saratoga, Oct. 17, 1777*. But most of the scenes that came off the stones and their coloring crew's worktable were contemporary to the mid-century. They included at least one view of a baseball game, several prints of trains and sailing ships, men at occupations such as whaling, firefighting, and blacksmithing, a few biblical scenes, and finally, some editorial cartoons.

Currier and Ives were the publishers, not the artists. Ives may have created some of the less colorful originals, but it appears that Currier could scarcely draw.

Cutting ice to store for summer.

He did pose for artists from time to time, but otherwise he worked long and hard at printing the lithographs, packing them for mailing throughout the world, and at all the other chores that made the business profitable.

Few of the prints were lithographed in color. Most came off the stone outlined in black. Women employees, sometimes as many as 12, would add the color, following a sample provided by the original artist. Some of the artists must have despaired to see almost every print come out with the same hues—harsh green and red, pale blue —that became the color trademark of a Currier and Ives print.

A brush for the lead; New York "Flyers" on the snow.

Currier & Ives

Toward the end of the century newspapers became much more numerous, and photography was well on its way to replacing the artist as a journalist. Nathaniel Currier retired in 1880 and died in 1888. James Ives

died in 1895. Both were succeeded by sons, but young Currier and Ives sold out their interests, and in 1907 the new owner went out of business. He sold the stones by the pound, an ignominious end to a whopping depository of 19th-century Americana.

Although but a few prints of Currier and Ives were on a Christmas theme, their winter scenes have long been used to illustrate Christmas. Some are used or imitated to illustrate Christmas cards and catalogs. One that is used frequently is a well-dressed couple riding in an open sleigh behind two spirited horses. The models for the original were Nathaniel Currier and his wife, Lura.

Another Currier and Ives print shows children gathering small Christmas trees. One of the most universal of our Christmas traditions today, the decorated tree was branded as pagan as late as 1851, and was not used much. Undoubtedly primitive peoples did use trees for rites and symbolism, but there is a clear history of the Christmas tree developing as a tradition on its own merits. In parts of northern Europe, people brought branches of trees indoors just before the first frost. They selected trees that would blossom, such as cherry and hawthorn, soaked them in water, and kept them warm near the stove or fireplace. Often they would blossom by Christmastime. The next step was to bring evergreens indoors at Christmas and decorate them to achieve the color and brightness of a blossoming tree.

There are a few loosely documented accounts of how the Christmas tree appeared in America. One attributes the first tree to Hessian soldiers during the Revolution. Perhaps, for the obvious reason, the Hessian custom was not welcomed at the time by the rebelling colonists. A professor of German at Harvard, Charles Follen, was reported to have set up an ever-

Currier & Ives

47

Christmas and skating go together.

Currier & Ives

green in his home in 1832, decorated with dolls, bright ornaments, and lighted candles. The next mention credits August Imgard of Wooster, Ohio, with decorating a small spruce outside his home in 1847.

Then, in 1851, Pastor Henry Schwan decorated a tree for his church in Cleveland. (He was obliged to cite his research and convince his congregation that the use of the tree was a Christian rite, not pagan.) He succeeded, and shortly after that the use of decorated evergreens spread rapidly, first to churches, then to homes.

Caroling at Christmas also is almost universal, and we tend to attribute the custom to "Merrie England." However, there is a strong indication that caroling actually began in Italy, where it was initiated by St. Francis of Assisi. Famous as the friend of birds, St. Francis is known in Greccio, Italy, as "father of the Christmas carol."

It seems to be a tradition, too, to decry some of the gaudier aspects of Christmas observances. The Pilgrim fathers firmly believed that to celebrate was to violate the spirit of Christmas. The General Court of Massachusetts in 1659 passed an edict forbidding anyone to miss his day's work on December 25th. A fine of five

shillings was levied against those who disobeyed, especially if they had been caught feasting or caroling.

Nowadays some Americans feel that the religious significance of Christmas suffers from too much commercialism. Some deplore the "garish" lighting of houses, the numerous Santa Clauses in stores and on the streets, and the practice of mailing printed greetings to a "list" instead of sending personal greetings to individuals. Many of us resent the hucksterism of retail merchants who commence in early November to advertise gift items and to proclaim "Open Every Nite 'Til Xmas."

But Christmas is a religious and a family day, and on Christmas Eve store managers and employees alike join the multitude coming home for Christmas.

The garish house lights seem to take on a warmer quality. Family groups sit around the pile of cards they've received over the past weeks and exchange memories of the friends who sent them. From midnight Christmas Eve to noon Christmas Day, churches are filled at their various services. Each pastor must surely note some almost forgotten faces, but nevertheless he is happy that his church family, too, is home for an old-time Christmas.

Hans Christian Andersen porcelain figurine
designed by Henning Seidelin for Bing and Grøndahl

Hans Christian Andersen

1805 - 1875

MELVA ROREM

With his wonderful smile, Hans Christian Andersen, master teller of his fairy tales, would gather the wide-eyed children around him for a story hour. Sometimes they would come singly, sometimes they would surround him in flocks. And it seemed that he literally breathed into them the charm and fantasy of his wonder stories, told with such delicate humor, such gentle truth. They responded with complete attention and respect. Affectionately, they called him Uncle Hans.

Denmark is a low-lying country with undulating plains, and softly rolling hills, and a wealth of lakes. And this Danish countryside, this veritable fairyland in which Hans Andersen grew up, seemed to enhance the enchantment of his tales. There are winding roads that lead to woods and copses and scented fields, where, his stories tell, such magic folk as mermaids, elves, trolls, and sprites live all year round.

Home for the boy Hans was the humble cottage where his father, Cobbler Andersen, pursued his shoemaker's trade in the quiet village of Odense. Here his mother went out and did washings (standing up to her knees in cold river water), kept the house spotless, cooked coarse-meal porridge every day, and brooded tenderly over her loved ones.

When Hans' wooden shoes beat fast on the wet cobbles in the street, his arms and legs churned in the air in a burst of joy; his shock of yellow hair jerked backward, and his mother would call to him, "Come, Small Yellow Head!" His father called him "Little Rabbit," and at night when the boy's silvery laughter rang through the cottage as he talked of simple joys of the day, the father's tired eyes brightened and found new life. On Sundays and holidays in the summer, father and son roamed the woods together, stopping to rest at favorite spots where they

49

would lose themselves in tales they loved—*The Arabian Nights,* Holberg's plays, and other classics.

When his *bedstemoder* (his beloved grandmother) visited them on Sundays, she always brought lovely flowers from gardens she tended. Hans Christian was allowed to arrange them in vases and place them about the room. His big awkward hands could do unbelievably delicate things with great beauty. He could cut paper lace, dress puppets, make bouquets and garlands. In fact, one of the last stories about him tells of his decorating a chair with flowers for his hostess's silver wedding day, insisting, in spite of weakness, on doing the whole job himself.

Hans' parents were so desperately poor that when they began keeping house they had to make most of their furniture. Even after their son was born, they had only one room and a tiny kitchen. In his autobiography Hans wrote: "Our one little room had nearly all the space filled up with the shoemaker's bench, the bed, and the folding crib on which I slept. The walls were covered with pictures and over the workbench was a cupboard containing books and songs; the little kitchen had a row of shining pewter plates, and the small space seemed big and rich to me."

When the bed curtains were drawn they seemed to make a little house, but through them Hans could see the firelight and hear his father reading. He would lie, half awake and half asleep, letting the words sink deep into his consciousness, feeling all the while that this room was the safest, happiest place on earth. As a child and as a man, the amiable Danish temperament—a lack of pretentiousness, a sweet reasonableness, and a joyful interpretation of life —was deeply imbedded in him.

And yet, with all the happy qualities the Danes exude, there is something else. Under the smiles there is an elusive sadness, a pensive brooding. And this melancholia did not escape Hans Andersen. "With a heart so beautiful, he will suffer much," one of his first teachers said.

When the mysterious, complex moods descended, Hans climbed the ladder to the red-tiled roof and stretched out under the blue sky. After a time of solitude his troubles would begin to fade away, and his spirit would sail away on some enticing cloud. Or, better yet, his vivid imagination would let him drift out into the world on a scarlet carpet to seek bags of gold so his parents would never be poor again.

Well, there is a sense in which this is what he really did.

In King's Garden at Copenhagen (the garden surrounds the castle of Rosenborg where generations of happy children have played) there is a statue of Hans Andersen reading. The statue is so life-like that the figure seems to speak—perhaps the beginning words from his little classic, "The Ugly Duckling":

The country was very lovely just then—it was summer. The wheat was golden and the oats still green. The hay was stacked in the rich low meadows, where the stork marched about on his long red legs, chattering Egyptian, the language his mother had taught him.

On one side of the base is a scene from this fairy tale. It captures the moment when the duckling, grown to full size, looks into the water and sees himself a swan.

"Life itself is the most wonderful fairy tale of all," he wrote. And, indeed, in his own life "the ugly duckling" was transformed into a swan.

As a growing boy, Hans looked strange indeed in his long coat, wooden shoes, and a cap with a broken peak. People laughed at his gawky awkwardness, his habit of shutting his eyes when he was in deep thought, and his wild, sometimes constant chattering that was hard to understand. He was lonely; no one seemed to understand him. He knew what it meant to be rebuffed and pushed and jeered, to be weary and downcast and abandoned, to struggle upward and fall, and then to climb again. But even when he met unkindness and ridicule, though he was deeply wounded by it, he forged ahead. He wrote plays, songs, fairy tales. He acted, danced, sang. He went to Copenhagen to study dancing and singing; later, he spent three years at grammar school at Slagelse.

Hans Andersen's writing continued. He was articulate and insisted on reading his works to everyone who would listen. At 23, he passed the difficult entrance examination to the University of Copenhagen, and a year later he passed the second examination, thereby completing his formal education. "Fairy Tales for Children," his first book, was published in 1835 when he was nearly 30.

Readers of that day found that a sentence from one of Hans Andersen's stories was utterly different from a sentence by any other writer. "It isn't writing, it's talking," one critic said. It almost seemed that a new prose was born in Danish literature; the language acquired grace and color and the freshness of simplicity. He took some of the stories from Danish folklore. Some tales are completely original, and some are an artistic blend of the two. They were written simply, just the way one would talk to a child. But Andersen felt that when parents read them to their children there must be some thoughts for the parents too. That is why children love them when they are little, and then find that when they read them again when they are grown, the stories have grown up right along with them.

In describing Andersen's writing, Rummer Godden writes: "In the Bible we are told that God formed man out of the dust of the earth and breathed into his nostrils . . . and man became a living soul. Without irreverence it might be said that Hans Andersen did something like that too; he formed his stories of

SKAGERRAK

KATTEGAT

•Århus

JUTLAND

SJAELLAND

•Odense

Hans Christian Andersen's home

Copenhagen
Ô

Roskilde Cathedral
Burial place of
Danish kings

FYN

GERMANY

the dust of the earth: a daisy, an old street lamp, a darning needle, a beetle, and made them live. His breath was unique; it was an alchemy of wisdom, poetry, honor, and innocence. . . . He was an adult, a lovable man. . . . He was a poet. . . . He was a child."

From 1835 until his death in 1875, he published more than 30 books. The pension he received from the state, honoring him as a writer, added to his earnings from his writings, and brought a measure of ease and comfort. His name became a household word among children as he traveled through his native land. Later, when the king awarded him a grant for travel, he visited the countries and people of Europe about which he had read and talked and dreamed. In awe he visited their cathedrals; his eager steps took him through their museums; he wandered ecstatically among the great works of their sculptors and painters. He hobnobbed with great authors: Balzac, Bjørnson, Dumas, Victor Hugo, Charles Dickens.

Andersen never married; the girls he loved married somebody else, and the one he loved best, the singer Jenny Lind, treated him as a dear brother. But at last "the awkward, fumbling creature at which all the barnyard had laughed," became a serene, stately swan. Even so, Hans Andersen never thought of himself as great; he was still, in a sense, the poor boy from Odense who wore a strange, long coat and wooden shoes — always grateful for every kindness, always grateful for every smile.

Hans had indeed been "the ugly duckling." Perhaps he had been his own little match-seller too, lighting matches that brought him sudden glows of imaginative warmth and comfort and visions of happiness.

> Quickly, quickly, another taper! And in a flash the little match girl found herself sitting under the most beautiful Christmas tree with thousands of candles burning on the branches. How warm and bright they were! She stretched her arms up to them and when the match went out, found them still shining above her in the stars high over her head. . . .

Hans, too, had often been left standing outside, shivering and alone. And his glowing imagination protected him from the cold experiences in his life and brought him to warmth. "She was trying to get warm," they said when they found her frozen body the next morning beside the used-up matches. But Hans Andersen added, "Nobody knew what lovely things she had seen and in what glory she had gone."

And was Hans perhaps "the little mermaid" too? "A mermaid hasn't any tears," he wrote, "and so she suffers all the more." Today her statue stands on the shores of the Langelinie—an exquisite bronze figure on a rock. Her face turns away from the busy, happy people on land. She looks ineffably lonely as she gazes out to the far stretching sea. Is she the personification of Andersen's lonely, searching heart?

An old, wise woman prophesied, when Hans was yet an ungainly boy whose strange, delicate ideas puzzled everyone, "He will be a wild bird who shall fly high, great and noble in the world. One day the whole of Odense will be illuminated for him."

Sixty years later her prediction came true. Hans Christian Andersen returned to Odense to be saluted as its first citizen. Every house was decorated in his honor, and a sea of bright flags and banners waved in the sun. Horsemen in bright red jackets and gleaming helmets galloped out to meet him while their leader said: "Hans Christian Andersen, the people of Odense await your coming with thanksgiving. This place of your birth, whose name you have made famous round the world, gives into your hands the keys of the city."

Hans leaned from his carriage window, waving and smiling. His eyes were on the children, and their high, clear voices were like music, calling out to him as they waved their tiny flags. "Uncle Hans! Uncle Hans! I'm here, Uncle Hans!"

"Oh, my pretty dears," he murmured as he waved.

Twilight deepened into night as Hans rode through the city streets. Up to the balcony of the old city hall he climbed. The big square below was ablaze with flaming torches. Hundreds of children marched round and round in a giant circle, singing his own lovely hymn to Denmark: "In Denmark I was born. . . ."

As the last tones wafted to the stars, an even greater bonfire was lighted in the center of the square, and as they raised their torches the crowd cheered again and again: "Andersen! Hans Andersen! Long live Hans Christian Andersen!"

And the guest of honor bowed his head with the deep-set eyes, and the curly hair, and the great forehead, and said, "Thank you, God. You have been so kind to me all my long years."

Hans Christian Andersen died peacefully August 4, 1875. At his funeral flowers were strewn up the center aisle of the church as if it were a wedding. For did not this event, too, hold promise of a new beginning?

He is buried in Copenhagen. But rather than visiting his grave, his fondest admirers linger at King's Garden at his eloquent reading statue and on the shores of the Langelinie where *The Little Mermaid* gazes out to sea. And so many visitors ask for directions to the Odense Museum, the house where he was born, that besides painting the kilometers to Svendborg and Nyborg and Bogense, there is an extra arm on the red and white signpost that reads: *Til H. C. Andersen's Hus.*

In Hans Andersen's story, "The Last Dream of the Oak Tree," the oak and the mayfly talk of death, when life will be over.

"Over, what is over?" asks the little fly. "Will all the beauty in the world die when you die?" she asks the tree.

"It will last longer, infinitely longer than I am able to imagine. . . ."

Child Jesus

Barn Jesus

Hans Christian Andersen, 1805-1875
Tr. Frank Pooler

Niels Gade, 1817-1890
Arr. Austin C. Lovelace

1. Child Je-sus in a man-ger lay, in sta-ble dark and lone,___ his
Barn Je-sus i en Kryb-be laa, skjønt Him-len var hans Ej - e, hans
2. Let ev-'ry gloom-y soul re-joice and cast out bit-ter pain.___ A

hum-ble pil-low coarse with hay, yet heav-en was his own.___ And
Pu-de her blev Hø og Straa, Mørkt var det om hans Lej - e; men
child is born in Da-vid's town to make us whole a - gain.___ So

o'er the town a star shone bright and ox-en kissed his feet that night. Al-
Stjer-nen o-ver Hus-et stod, og Ox-en kys-sed Bar-nets Fod. Hal-
let us to the Christ child go and sing from hearts that o - ver-flow. Al-

le - lu-ia! Al-le - lu-ia! Child Je - sus.
le - lu-ja! Hal-le - lu-ja! Barn Je - sus.
le - lu-ia! Al-le - lu-ia! Al-le - lu - ia!

Down to Earth, As a Dove

Fred Kaan

Robert Leaf

Christ is here, ev - er near! Glo — — ri-a in ex-

cel — sis. sis.

On This Day Is Born a Savior

Natalie Sleeth

Natalie Sleeth

♩ = 88

Ho - di - e Chris - tus na - tus est, ho - di - e in
On this day is born a Sav - ior, on this day in

It Came Upon the Midnight Clear

Edmund Hamilton Sears, 1810-1876   Richard Storrs Willis, 1819-1900

1. It came up-on the mid-night clear, that glo-rious song of old,
2. Yet with the woes of sin and strife the world has suf-fered long;
3. For lo, the days are has-tening on by proph-et-bards fore-told,

from an-gels bend-ing near the earth to touch their harps of gold:
be-neath the an - gel~strain have rolled two thou-sand years of wrong.
when, with the ev - er-cir-cling years, shall come the age of gold;

'Peace on the earth, good will to men, from heaven's all gra-cious King!'
And man, at war with man, hears not the love song which they bring:
when peace shall o - ver all the earth its heaven-ly splen-dors fling,

The world in sol-emn still-ness lay to hear the an - gels sing.
O hush the noise, ye men of strife, and hear the an - gels sing.
and all the world give back the song which now the an - gels sing.

Carol of the Birds

Traditional Catalonian
Tr. George K. Evans

Traditional Catalonian Carol
Arr. Robert Wetzler

Expressive

1. Up-on this ho-ly night, when God's great star ap-pears, and
   En veu-re des-pun-tar el ma-jor il-lu-mi-nar en
2. The par-tridge adds his note: To Beth-le-hem I'll fly, where

floods the earth with bright-ness, birds' voic-es rise in song, and,
la nit més joi-o-sa; els o-cel-lettes can-tant a
in the stall he's ly-ing. There, near the man-ger blest, I'll

warb-ling all night long, ex-press their glad hearts' light — ness.
fes-te-jar-lo van, amb sa veu — mel-in-dro — sa.
build my-self a nest, and sing my love un-dy — ing.

Text, Walter Ehret and George K. Evans, *The International Book of Christmas Carols*, © 1963. Reprinted by permission of Prentice-Hall, Inc., Englewood Cliffs, New Jersey. Arrangement copyright 1976 Augsburg Publishing House.

Birds' voic-es rise in song,_____ and, warb-ling all night
Els o-cel-lettes can - tant_____ a fes - te jar - lo
There, near the màn - ger blest,_____ I'll build my-self a

long, ex - press their glad hearts' light — ness._____
van amb-sa veu me - lin - dro - sa._____
nest, and sing my love un - dy - ing._____

Tribute to a Carol

Pablo Casals, 1876-1973, world-renowned cellist, whose life is a testament to his credo of "the invisible affinity between art and human values," said this about "Carol of the Birds":

The tale of the nativity has always had a special meaning for me.

One of the first compositions on which I worked—I was six or seven at the time—was the music my father and I wrote for a performance of *Els Pastorets*, the "Adoration of the Shepherds." The pageant took place at the Catholic Center in Vendrell, and I played the part of the devil, who plotted—devilishly, of course—all sorts of cunning schemes to prevent the shepherds and Wise Men from getting to Bethlehem.

More than 70 years later, when I was already living in exile from Spain after the Civil War, I began the custom of concluding concerts and music festivals with the melody of an old Catalan folk song which is actually a Christmas carol. It is called *El Cant del Ocells*, the "Song of the Birds." The melody then came to be known as the nostalgic theme of the Spanish refugees. Today in the village of Molitg-les-Bains in the French Pyrenees, adjoining the lovely spa of the Hotel Grand Thermal, I have a cottage at which I have stayed in recent years during the Prades music festivals. The owner of the hotel has placed a carillon of 15 bells in a tower there. I recorded the "Song of the Birds" for the bells, and every hour you can hear its haunting melody sing out, echoing among the mountains. On the largest bell is an inscription which says that through this song I speak of the sorrow and homesickness of Catalans. It adds, "May this be for them tomorrow—a song of peace and hope."

From *Joys and Sorrows: Reflections by Pablo Casals*, as told to Albert E. Kahn. Simon and Schuster, Inc., New York, 1970.

Puerto Rico News Service

Poems of Christmas

Song for Christmas Eve

Tonight it snowed.
Within the woods I walked while twilight fell.
Early white stars pierced earth with their blest
   miracle.
My heart caught magic from the night that it would
   tell.
Tonight it snowed.

Tonight it snowed.
The star and Child were more than sacred memory.
The soft, snow-wind of night became a rhapsody
That rose and fell again in liquid melody.
Tonight it snowed.

Tonight it snowed.
In silent, hidden woods my footsteps left scant trace.
The snowflakes, weaved from purified, transparent
   lace,
Melted—a kind of baptism upon my face.
Tonight it snowed.

Melva Rorem

That Holy Thing

They all were looking for a king
  To slay their foes and lift them high,
Thou cam'st, a little baby thing
  That made a woman cry.

O Son of man to right my lot
  Nought but thy presence can avail;
Yet on the road thy wheels are not,
  Nor on the seas thy sail!

My fancied ways why shouldst thou heed?
  Thou cam'st down thine own secret stair;
Cam'st down to answer all my need,
  Yes, every bygone prayer!

George MacDonald

First Christmas Eve

There were the silent things:
Compassion in Joseph's eyes,
Glory on Mary's face
Vaster than any skies,
And loveliness of grace.

There were the lowly things:
The manger bed of hay,
The stable narrow-aisled,
Shepherds who found the way
To the little Child.

There were the deathless things:
God's great eternal gift
Of life forevermore,
His shoreless love to lift
Each heart that breathes a prayer,
And shining peace to be
A bright infinity.

Grace V. Watkins

Followers

Lord,
it seems to me
one must be single-minded
to follow a star.
Wise Men
saw its signal in the east
and followed.
Even Herod could not sidetrack them
with doubts
or conflicting philosophies
along the way.
They felt an urgency,
a calling,
and in responding
found the King of kings.

We feel that sense of search,
that summoning,
in our time too, Lord,
and we long to follow.
Not a star,
announcing your arrival,
but you.

Jone Anderson

The Birds' Christmas Tree

GRACIA CHRISTENSEN
(A story for children, dedicated to my daughters)

Illustrated by Melva Mickelson

It was still a month until Christmas, but ten-year-old Tyrna was already excited. (Her name was really Thora, but she had called herself Tyrna when she first learned to talk, and had been known by that name ever since.) This morning, as she rocked little brother Johan in his cradle, she hoped he would sleep soon and long. For today was the day to trim the Birds' Christmas Tree!

At last he was asleep. Tyrna hurried to the large kitchen where mother was busily preparing the delicious jellied meat called "sylta," always a special Christmas treat.

"I'm ready to start! Jan is fast asleep," said Tyrna eagerly. Her brown braids danced and her brown eyes sparkled.

"Hurray!" said the three other children. "We waited for you as we promised."

At the square wooden table they now took their places, standing one at each side. Big-sister Ragnhild carefully held a sharp knife and began to cut neat pieces from a big chunk of suet. These she passed to Tyrna, who held a small round tool looking like a large nail, with which she made a hole through the middle of each piece. Little-sister Anna had an assort-

ment of colored string, cut into short lengths. For each piece of suet she chose a piece of string, whatever color she wished. Then brother Peder put the string she had selected through the suet hole and tied the ends in a secure knot. And soon there was quite a good-sized pile of finished pieces lying on the table.

"Let's count how many there are," suggested Peder.

So he took a long smooth stick, and gave it to Ragnhild and Tyrna, one end to each. Anna picked up the pieces of suet, one by one, and gave them to Peder. He in turn hung them on the stick the girls held.

"One, two, three," the children counted, in great merriment. The more they counted, the louder grew their voices.

"Sh-h-h," warned mother. "You'll wake up Jan."

The counting continued in a whisper. "Thirteen, fourteen, fifteen. . . ." The red and green and yellow strings hung side by side on the stick, with the good, fresh suet dangling from each string. Peder kept adding until the whole pile was gone.

"Forty pieces," he said then. "Forty pieces, mama!"

"Good," answered mother, smiling into the glad eyes of the children. "Now see how many more you can make from the scraps that are left."

The Birds' Tree had been selected weeks before—a thick, bushy-branched fir tree, not much taller than Tyrna. It stood some yards from the house, on a patch of ground high above the fjord below. Beyond this patch of ground a rocky hill tumbled down almost to the edge of the water. Stretching down the hill was a well-worn footpath, with a smooth, sturdy handrail alongside it. But the danger of the deep, cold fjord waters was so great that the children were never allowed to go down there alone. On the other side of the house were plenty of fields for playing, and paths for walking, and there they found much to do. This year the little fir tree on the fjord side had grown to be so beautiful, however, that they had honored it by choosing it as the Birds' Christmas Tree. Father had heartily agreed, too, for it stood a safe distance back from the steep hill.

When the stringing of the suet was finished, the children put on their warm clothing and marched joyously outside. Peder was first, as the man of the party. Then came Tyrna and Ragnhild, carrying the well-filled stick between them. And lastly little Anna trudged happily behind them. It was a clear, beautiful day, with very little snow, and even mildness in the air.

"Where are the birds?" asked Anna, looking around.

"Waiting for us to get something ready to coax them here," answered Peder readily. "Now we start! You're first, Anna!"

Anna took off one mitten so she could better remove a bright green string from the stick. The little square of suet at the end of the string seemed to dance with excitement, and Anna waved it round and round. With Peder's help she slipped it over the fir needles, as high up as she could reach, and tightened the string, so the birds could peck at the suet without knocking it off the branch.

"Now for a wish," cried the children all together. Each one must always make a wish with the first piece he hung on the Birds' Tree. Anna closed her eyes tightly and made believe she was thinking hard. Actually, of course, the wish was thought out and decided long before this.

"I wish I could see so many birds on our tree all at once that there would be one eating at every piece of suet at the same time," she announced firmly.

"That's a good wish," said Peder, proudly. "Now here goes for my piece." A yellow string was soon tied tightly around a low branch and Peder straightened up.

"I wish I wouldn't see a single bird fight on our Tree this year," he said simply. Peder was a gentle boy, and hated all forms of quarrelling, even among the birds.

Ragnhild chose a red-stringed piece for hers. She wished that she might awaken every morning to the sound of birds singing or chattering in the Tree. Ragnhild and Tyrna had the front bedroom upstairs, in direct view of the fjord and the Tree.

Next Tyrna tied her suet to the Tree and then turned seriously to her brother and sisters.

"I have thought a long time about my wish," she said, so solemnly that they stared at her. "I wish it more than any other wish, and so I'm going to make it. *I wish I could see the Christ child when he blesses our Birds' Tree.*"

"Tyrna!" whispered the others, shocked, looking instinctively toward the house to see if Mother had heard. "Tyrna! What have you said?"

Tyrna's brown eyes were not at all disturbed.

"I didn't mean anything wrong. Everyone knows the Christ child must bless the Birds' Tree. I wish, wish, wish that I could see him when he does. So that's my wish, isn't it?"

The children returned to their happy task, and soon the little tree stood decked in its gifts of love and care for the birds. Never must the dumb creatures be forgotten in the holy Christmas season! This lesson every boy and girl learned in Norway.

Late that night, when the moon had risen high, and the Birds' Tree was beautiful in the silver light, the heavy latch of the front door was raised. Mother awakened suddenly and lay listening in the dark stillness. Surely she had heard the door opening? She arose quietly and tiptoed downstairs. The front door stood ajar, and there a startling sight met her eyes. Tyrna was walking slowly toward the Tree, with her arms wide open as if to welcome someone. She was dressed only in her long flannel nightgown, and in the knitted booties everyone wore to bed at night to keep feet warm.

Mother was about to call out sharply when the truth dawned suddenly upon her. Tyrna was walking in her sleep! Once before the little girl had been found wandering around during the night on an upstairs porch. She had been suddenly wakened that time and badly frightened, and had been so upset by the experience that she was seriously ill afterwards. Lest this happen again, mother now ran quickly upstairs and woke father, who could best handle Tyrna. He threw on his shoes and coat and rushed to the door. But outside Tyrna was nowhere to be seen. The little Tree stood alone in the glistening moonlight.

Thoroughly alarmed, father ran to the edge of the steep, plunging hill. And there, already far down on the path, was the little night-clad figure, walking firmly and quickly, her arms still outstretched.

"She must be half frozen with cold," thought father, his heart aching and afraid. "O God, help me to reach her before she reaches the fjord." Grasping the handrail securely, he started after her with long, yet almost noiseless steps.

But she reached the bottom well before him. As was customary in Norway, there was a narrow plank jutting out into the fjord-waters, used for tying up rowboats. Upon this plank Tyrna now set her feet, and father could hardly repress a great cry when he saw her begin to walk out. What could he now do? The plank was not wide enough for them both. The water was deep, and so cold. . . .

Father prayed in anguish for God's help, as his last long leap brought him to the water's edge. And then a miracle happened. Tyrna's extended arms dropped stiffly to her side, and slowly she began to *back up* to the shore! There she stood, a forlorn little figure, facing the black waters of the fjord, with the wind whipping at her long nightgown and the moon spilling silver all around her. Father was shaking, his heart pounding, but very quietly he touched her hand, turned her around, and gently led her all the way back up the hill to the house.

She was still fast asleep when father and mother placed her in her bed, warmed with hot stones wrapped in thick blanket-pieces. They put an extra feather tick over her. And they prayed that God who had so wonderfully saved her this night would now guard her from serious illness.

63

The next morning Tyrna was feverish and unwell. But she seemed strangely happy nevertheless.

"Ragnhild," she confided to her sister, "I dreamed that my wish came true! Oh, it was a wonderful, wonderful dream! The Christ child *did* bless our Birds' Tree. You can't imagine how beautiful he was. I followed him when he left, right down the hill. I wanted to follow him across the fjord, but he said I couldn't come, this time. He even pushed me back, very, very gently. I watched him walk across the water until a great light took him away."

Unknown to Tyrna, father stood in the doorway listening, his face pale and drawn. Now he hurried to her bedside and held the hot hands in his cold ones.

"What are you saying, little Tyrna? Do you know that last night we found you walking in your sleep again? You walked down the hill, right to the edge of the fjord."

Tyrna looked at her father thunderstruck. Then her brown eyes lighted with more than the light of the fever, and she asked eagerly: "Did I walk out on the boat plank, too?"

"Yes," answered father, shuddering at the memory. But Tyrna was jubilant.

"Then it wasn't a dream! It was real! Ragnhild, Peder, Anna! My wish came true! *I saw the Christ child bless our Birds' Tree!*"

Long years afterwards, far from the Norway fjords, Tyrna told the strange story to her own children, as I am telling it to you now. And someday you in turn may tell your children, too, about your grandmother Tyrna, and the Birds' Christmas Tree.

WITH THE TELLING OF A STORY
(To Mother)

Grandma was
a lady in a photograph from nineteen-six
whom I looked at, respectfully;
then forgot in play.
Dead three months before my birth,
she was, to my child mind,
a simile: *like* something, someone.
More, "grandma" was
a foreign word—touchstone of another world,
a word like "God."

Then you told me "The Birds' Christmas Tree."
On memory's evergreen
you hung suet of true happenings,
tied with the bright colors
of your words and phrases.

Suddenly, grandma was
not just a lady in high-necked wedding dress
boxed forever in a picture frame.
Freed from a postured stance—left hand
on the shoulder of a moustached man,
she ran and clapped her hands
. . . and walked that awful plank.
Alice-like,
grandma shrank—not in size, but years;
became Tyrna, a child like me.

Her smile trapped no longer in a camera's blink,
she laughed out loud with glee
at the Birds' Christmas Tree.
Her brown eyes, now no mere paper dots, shone:
they had seen the Christ child!

Thus, with the telling of a story, mother—
with your verbal trimming of a Birds' Christmas Tree,
you too are handmaid to the miracle
of spirit *come alive* in a child's eyes.

NADIA CHRISTENSEN

64

A Man of Goodwill

Albert Schweitzer (1875-1965)

*Peace upon earth
among men of goodwill!*

LAWRENCE W. DENEF

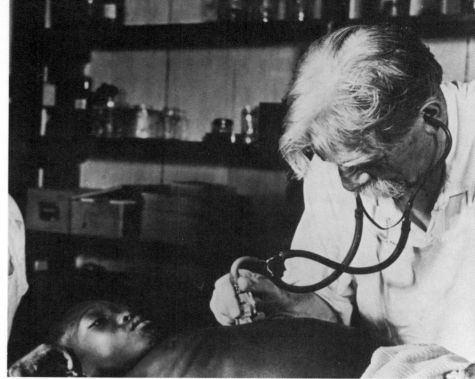

A quiet ministry in a jungle hospital

Several years ago Albert Schweitzer was universally acclaimed as "a godly man in the midst of a godless age," a "contemporary saint," the "most significant moral philosopher of our century." Today the man we said he was has all but been forgotten, and the legacy he left, lost on the pages of innumerable books no longer in print. Even the 100th anniversary of the birth of this "friend of humanity" recently passed without significant public comment.

Perhaps our loss of memory has been occasioned by the very spirit of our times which Albert Schweitzer, according to his own testimony, so vehemently opposed. At any rate it is precisely Schweitzer's opposition to what he called this "suicidal spirit" which continues to make him and his message relevant.

From his autobiography we learn that already as a student Schweitzer was appalled by the "spiritual fatigue" he found evidenced everywhere.

> As early as my first years at the University, I had begun to feel misgivings about the opinion that mankind is constantly developing in the direction of progress. My impression was that the fire of its ideals was burning low. . . . On a number of occasions I had to acknowledge that public opinion . . . approved of as opportune inhuman courses of action taken by governments and nations. . . . I had to infer the growth of a peculiar intellectual and spiritual fatigue in this generation which is so proud of what it has accomplished.[1]

This impression gradually led him to the conclusion that our civilization was no longer safe because it had developed much greater vigor materially than it had spiritually.

> Through the discoveries which subject the powers of nature to us in such a remarkable way the living conditions of individuals, of groups, and of states have been completely revolutionized. Our knowledge and consequent power are enriched and enhanced to an unbelievable extent; and thus we are in a position to frame the conditions of man's existence incomparably more favorably in many respects than was previously possible. But in our enthusiasm for knowledge and power we have arrived at a mistaken conception of what civilization is. We overvalue the material gains wrung from nature, and have no longer present in our minds the true significance of the spiritual element in life. And now come the stern matters of fact which call us to reflect. They teach us in terms of awful severity that a civilization which develops itself on the material, and not in a corresponding degree on the spiritual side, is like a ship with defective steering gear, which becomes more unsteerable from moment to moment, and so rushes on to catastrophe.[2]

It was to avoid this catastrophe that Schweitzer devoted himself and his work.

> A new Renaissance must come, and a much greater one than that which we stepped out of the Middle Ages; a great Renaissance in which mankind discovers that the ethical is the highest truth and the highest practicality. . . . I would be a humble pioneer of this Renaissance, and throw the belief in a new humanity like a torch into our dark age.[3]

This vision of a new humanity living seriously the religion of love and actualizing it, defending it against all opposition, practicing it in the dailiness of decision making and priority setting—this vision of what it means to be truly human has rightfully become the lasting legacy of the man from Lambaréné.

Theologian, pastor, philosopher, accomplished composer, organist, medical doctor, missionary, architect, husbandman, administrator — Schweitzer appears at first to be a universal genius, at home in several entirely different areas of human endeavor. But upon closer scrutiny one soon discovers that all of these divergent, seemingly independent activities, actually form an organic unity. Like the spokes of a wheel they emanate from a common center, and in this case that center is the ethical imperative which can best be expressed by the phrase "reverence for life." Schweitzer's greatness lies precisely in this singularity of vision. Nothing other than a lifetime devoted to the comprehension, expression, and emerging realization of this single idea can explain the remarkable effectiveness of Albert Schweitzer. Once deeply experienced, "reverence for life" became the dominant motif of his life.

Albert Schweitzer was born on January 14, 1875, in the Alsatian countryside of Germany and spent his younger years in a parsonage at Günsbach. Even then he tells us he was already troubled by the cruelty he saw, and when evening prayers were said he would add his own little prayer: "Protect and bless all things that have breath; guard them from all evil, and let them sleep in peace."

Young Schweitzer entered this world as a delicate child but soon began to develop normally. He was never a model student, nor did he excel in any of the subjects he was required to take during his elementary school years. Music was the one exception. It was his earliest passion. By five he was receiving piano lessons from his father, and even before his legs were long enough to reach the pedals, he was at the organ. At nine he was already substituting for the regular organist at the Günsbach church.

For Schweitzer music was an intrinsic necessity of life. Even in later years, under tremendous pressures of time, every free moment was devoted to mastering this "queen of the arts." During his early studies he was introduced to the music of Bach, and took private organ lessons from the distinguished Parisian organist Charles Marie Widor. Within several years the student himself would become an expert at the organ, a recitalist in universal demand, and eventually the renowned author of several works on Johann Sebastian Bach. But his love for this great master of music went far beyond scholastic insights and original interpretations. Young Schweitzer also took practical steps to restore and maintain the old church organs on which Bach himself had played, and championed the revival of the honored craft of organ construction at every opportunity.

Certainly Schweitzer could have found his life's fulfillment as a musician. But sometime between the ages of 14 and 16 he had already come to the firm conclusion that "reason" was a necessary ingredient of all normal spiritual progress; or to use his own words, "All real progress in the world is in the last analysis produced by rationalism." "Actually I have remained what I had then already become," Schweitzer later asserted. And so following his graduation from high school it was not to music but to the faculties of "reason" that he dedicated himself, and entered into his studies in philosophy and theology at Strassburg.

During this period in his life another insight won a prominent place in his thinking: "It became ever clearer to me, that I did not have the inner right to take for granted my happy childhood, my health, and my power to work. Anyone who is spared personal suffering is called upon to empathise with, to help and to alleviate the suffering of others." This insight led Schweitzer to another significant decision: Until the age of 30 he would concentrate on developing his own potential: pursue scholastic achievement, cultivate his musical talent, and enter the office of the pastoral ministry. Then, upon reaching his 30th year, he would dedicate himself entirely and wholeheartedly to the immediate and direct service of people in need.

In accordance with this remarkable decision (he was only 21 at the time), Schweitzer plunged into his studies with enthusiasm. In 1899 he earned his doctor of philosophy degree with a dissertation on "Kant's Philosophy of Religion." After completing his first theological examination, he accepted the call as pastor of St. Nicolai in Strassburg. One year later he received his doctorate in theology.

During the succeeding years it was theology that became Schweitzer's greatest love and the focal point of his attention. Concentrating on the problems raised by the liberal theologians of his time and their quest for a true picture of the historical Jesus, he attempted to describe the various points of view from which the life of Jesus had been viewed, in order himself to formulate a clearer understanding of who Jesus really was. But the further he probed into the problem the more he began to realize that a historical reconstruction of the life of Jesus was impossible. In fact, what was needed, he discovered, was not some restored image of the Jesus behind Scriptures but a direct unmediated faith response to the Jesus who comes to us as he once came to the very people portrayed in Scriptures. The concluding paragraph in his monumental work, "The Quest of the Historical Jesus," is still as powerful in its impact as when it was first written.

> "He comes to us as One unknown, without a name, as of old, by the lakeside, He came to those men who knew Him not. He speaks to us the same word: 'Follow thou me!' and sets us to the tasks which He has to fulfill in our time. He commands. And to those who obey Him, whether they be wise or simple, He will reveal Himself in the toils, the conflicts, the sufferings which they shall pass through in His fellowship, and, as an ineffable mystery, they shall learn in their own experience who He is."

During the years that Schweitzer devoted all of his time to music and scholarly studies in philosophy and theology, he never forgot his decision to give up these personal pursuits and enter into the service of suffering human beings. Upon reaching his 30th year, he did as he had determined he would, by making tentative beginnings in a ministry to the imprisoned. But as the months passed he grew increasingly restless and dissatisfied with himself and his accomplishments. Quite by accident one morning in the fall of 1904 he picked up a magazine published by the Parisian Evangelical Mission Society and glanced through an article depicting the misery of the black people in the region of the African Congo and their urgent need for medical attention. The moment he lifted his eyes from the page he knew what he had to do; soon thereafter he began his third academic pursuit—medicine.

His decision raised the eyebrows of the academic community. Despite their snide jibes, Schweitzer completed his new studies, putting in innumerable late night hours sustained by coffee and cold water. After receiving a doctor of medicine degree in February of 1913, there was little that could hold him in Europe. He spent one month packing some 70 cases of items for the outfitting of a jungle hospital, and off he went on an adventure that was to last the remainder of his lifetime.

During the next years the world-renowned sick station of Lambaréné became a reality, rising slowly but surely out of the jungle swamps along the Ogowe river in what is now the African Republic of Gabon. Schweitzer the intellectual, together with his wife and a few native laborers, engaged in the task of building a hospital from scratch without previous experience and with hardly any outside help—not only once but again in 1924, and in 1927, each time enlarging and improving the previous compound — a remarkable, if not entirely miraculous accomplishment.

In 1917 Schweitzer was forced to leave his beloved Lambaréné. Brought back to Europe he was interned in a prison camp and kept under close scrutiny. The enforced exile proved beneficial, for Schweitzer employed every free moment not only to clarify his thought, but to perfect his organ technique. Using a small table as an imaginary manual and the floorboards as pedals, he practiced daily. And so, upon his release, he was able to do what he had always done during his European trips—schedule organ recitals and lectures wherever he went. These engagements, plus the charitable gifts of sympathetic friends, provided the sole source of funding for his African work, allowing him complete freedom and independence, unencumbered by the need for governmental support and its imposed regulations.

After 1924 Schweitzer spent more and more of his time in Lambaréné. There he earned the deep and abiding respect of the black Africans who affectionately called him "our white medicine man." His openness as a person and his skill as a doctor enabled him to alleviate the misery of many native blacks who suffered under a host of oppressive tropical diseases. As Lambaréné grew in prestige and the staff of medical personnel increased, Schweitzer devoted more and more time to administrative tasks—maintenance, development, expansion, renewal—and in the process became a rather resourceful and inventive manager. In a very real sense it was his singleness of vision, his devotion to helping others, his gifted ability for guidance in the accomplishment of necessary tasks, and his personal presence and example that made this mission in the Congo possible. Without Schweitzer there could have been no Lambaréné. It became the culmination of his life's work, the visible expression of his "reverence for life."

At his death in 1965 the hospital contained 20 large corrugated sheet-iron and bamboo cottages in which approximately 6500 patients were treated annually. And that number does not include the families who were always welcomed to accompany and care for their ill.

After Schweitzer's death, Lambaréné entered upon troubled times. Increasingly, personnel and financial problems began to weaken its organizational structure and limit the services offered. But these signs of decline were merely the outer expressions of a far deeper loss—the loss of the man Schweitzer and his vision. Lambaréné was unique because Albert Schweitzer was unique. With the passing of Schweitzer it was almost inevitable that Lambaréné would enter troubled times.

The present situation is regrettable, not because Lambaréné maintained the memory of Albert Schweitzer, but because over the years it had become a universal symbol of respect for man's humanity. In the heart of the African jungle there was a place where suffering men, women, and children could find not merely healing but wholeness.

After World War I the works of Schweitzer began to receive worldwide acclaim. Honor upon honor was bestowed upon him. And in 1952 he received that most coveted of awards—the Nobel Peace Prize. But respect soon waned. Continuing to champion the preservation of life from his African outpost, he could not help but speak out anew against the increasing spread of nuclear weapons and the growing pollution of our universe. His words fell on deaf ears. Those who had never understood him sought to discredit everything he said, and those in power simply passed him by.

Albert Schweitzer died on September 4, 1965, a great "realist of the spirit" who courageously confronted the barbarism of our times, insisting that persons can no longer live for themselves alone, that immaculate self-centered perfection is not enough, and that each of us should in some way give ourselves as persons to others. "Reverence for life" is his lasting legacy. His life itself is our encouragement to try.

In a letter written when Schweitzer reached the age of 80, his friend and admirer Martin Buber wrote:

Dear Albert Schweitzer—

Since my earliest years it has been a great encouragement, and in later years a comforting thought, that people like you exist. As you know, I have always been concerned with those who help mankind, and you have been one of the great helpers in so many ways. Every time one man helps another, the *hasidim* say, an angel is born. I hope, my dear Albert Schweitzer, that fate will long allow you to hear the wings of many angels beating about you.

Yours,
Martin Buber[4]

[1] *Out of My Life and Thought* by Albert Schweitzer. Henry Holt and Co., 1933, New York. Translated by C. T. Campion, pp. 146f.
[2] *Civilization and Ethics*, Part II of *The Philosophy of Civilization* by Albert Schweitzer. Macmillan, 1929, New York. Translated by C. T. Campion, p. 2.
[3] *Civilization and Ethics*, p. 23.
[4] *Martin Buber: An Intimate Portrait* by Aubrey Hodes. Viking Press, 1971, New York, p. 152.

Volume I - 1931

Volume II - 1932

Volume III - 1933

Volume IV - 1934

Volume V - 1935

Volume VI - 1936

Volume VII - 1937

Volume VIII - 1938

Volume IX - 1939

Volume X - 1940

Volume XI - 1941

Volume XII - 1942

Volume XIII - 1943

Volume XIV - 1944

Volume XV - 1945

Christmas 1976

is a unique blend of yesterday and today. Through art, and literature, and music, Randolph E. Haugan, founder and editor of the volume, brings us again in this 46th edition to the overwhelming message of Christmas: "To you is born . . . a Savior." The type is set in Linotype Caledonia. Headings are set in Monotype Goudy Blackletter with Lombardic initials. *Christmas* is printed by photo-offset lithography and published by Augsburg Publishing House, Minneapolis, Minnesota.

Volume XVI - 1946

Volume XVII - 1947

Volume XVIII - 1948

Volume XIX - 1949

Volume XX - 1950

Volume XXI - 1951

Volume XXII - 1952

Volume XXIII - 1953

Volume XXIV - 1954

Volume XXV - 1955

Volume XXVI -1956

Volume XXVII - 1957

Volume XXVIII - 1958

Volume XXIX - 1959

Volume XXX - 1960

Volume XXXI - 1961

Volume XXXII - 1962

Volume XXXIII - 1963

Volume XXXIV - 1964

Volume XXXV - 1965

Volume XXXVI - 1966

Volume XXXVII - 1967

Volume XXXVIII - 1968

Volume XXXIX - 1969

Volume XL - 1970

Volume XLI - 1971

Volume XLII - 1972

Volume XLIII - 1973

Volume XLIV - 1974

Volume XLV - 1975